Granny's Stories

From Jamaica to England

Jade Calder & Alaya Haughton

Granny's Stories...From Jamaica to England

First published 2021 by Jade Calder Books
Copyright © 2021 Jade Calder & Alaya Haughton

All rights reserved.

No part of this publication may be reproduced, stored in a retrieval system, or transmitted, in any form or by any means, without the prior permission of the publisher, nor be otherwise circulated without the publisher's prior consent in any form of binding or cover other than that in which it is published and without a similar condition including this condition being imposed on the subsequent publisher.

The moral right of the author has been asserted.

Hardcover ISBN: 978 1 9169010 0 1
Paperback ISBN: 978 1 9169010 1 8
eBook ISBN: 978 1 9169010 2 5

Typesetting and formatting:
Beaten Track Publishing
www.beatentrackpublishing.com

FROM JAMAICA TO ENGLAND

Monday	🖌️	Paint
Tuesday	⚽	Football
Wednesday	ABC ✏️	Writing
Thursday	📚	Reading
Friday	Go to Granny's	🏠
Saturday	💤🐑	Coco + Cookies
Sunday	Chicken, Rice + Peas	

Alaia loved visiting her grandma. She would go to Granny's for sleepovers every weekend.

Granny had a strong Jamaican accent, and Alaia loved it, especially when Granny told stories from when she was a little girl.

Alaia would sit on Granny's lap and listen to all the stories with a plate of cookies and a nice cup of coco cooling on the coffee table.

On Sundays, Granny cooked her famous chicken, rice and peas.

It made the house smell so scrumptious.

Alaia also loved Granny's back garden, as Alaia only had a small backyard at her house.

In Granny's garden, there were beautiful flowers, a trampoline and a swing.

One of the special things at Granny's was her secret coco.

"Granny," said Alaia, "why do you boil the milk for the coco in the pan?"

"Dis is how we do it in Jamaica," said Granny. "We boil up di milk and add a secret ingredient."

"Ahhh!" said Alaia. "What is the secret ingredient?"

Granny burst out laughing. "Ha-ha-ha! Dat is why it is a secret! Mi can't tell you dat!"

"Your coco tastes different from Mum's. I like yours better," chuckled Alaia.

They both snuggled up on the sofa like they always did. Alaia was beaming with excitement, ready for another one of Granny's stories.

"OK, Alaia, which story you want to hear now? Mi know you want a story," said Granny, smiling.

"Well..." said Alaia, "can you tell me the one about when you first came to live in England?"

"You want dat one again?" Granny sighed.

Alaia nodded.

"OK, child, if you must..."

"It was January 1967. Me and mi eldest sister and mi eldest brother..." Granny paused.

"When we get di news dat we had to come to England, I hid mi passport form so I dint have to come."

"I neva wanted to leave mi grandmama. But it neva work. Dey went and get mi a new form from di airport."

"As di plane came in to land, I look out and see snow. I neva see it before!

"When mi get off di plane, it was like stepping out of an oven into a freezer."

Alaia shuffled up closer and pulled the blanket over her toes.

"Carry on, Granny," she said.

"Yes, mi dear. So when I came here, every ting was different. It was cold and it smell of smoke..."

"...not like back home, where it was sunshine and mango hanging off di tree in di garden. I have some pictures you can look at..."

"I couldn't believe it. I was shocked!" said Granny.

"When I went to school, I was twelve years old, so I went straight to high school. I had a big, big Afro."

"Most of di girls were friendly to me. They all loved mi accent."

"I also use to mek mi own clothes for mi dolly and mi family of ten children."

"Wow!" said Alaia.

"TEN brothers and sisters! That's a lot!"

"Yes, mi dear," Granny agreed.

"Back home, we lived in a big house with a veranda looking out over a big field."

"When I seen di new house in England, it was a lot smaller than di one back home."

"Dey had chimneys and were all close together."

"On mi fourth day back from school, mi get lost. I decided to follow mi friends to di shops in town and take a different route home."

"Dey jump on di bus. I neva knew where I was going.

"Dey leave me at di bus stop after we get back from the shops."

"I walk up and down di roads, but mi just could not find mi way back."

Alaia was amazed. Granny laughed.

"Yes, I had to ask a policeman on di street if he could help mi find mi way back home."

"Did he help you?"

"Yes," said Granny. "I remembered di street name, and he took mi back home. Luckily, he knew where he was going."

"When mi mother saw di police turn up at di front door, she said, 'Officer, what eva it was she did, she is innocent!'" Granny smiled, remembering. "Mummy always stuck up for her children."

"And di police officer – he laughed and said, 'She hasn't done any ting apart from get lost on her way back from school!'"

Alaia giggled. "That's funny!"

"It was funny indeed!" said Granny, edging forward off the sofa.

"All right, petal, it's time for bed."

"Can I have one more story? Please, please, please…"

"Tomorrow," said Granny, laughing at Alaia's pleading.

"Der's plenty more," she said, and she hugged Alaia and kissed her on her forehead.

"OK. Just one more. One time, mi brother and sisters and I were playing in di park. Mi brother throw di ball, and it hit a dog. Di dog chased us... We all ran, and I fell down. Di dog jump on mi and bite mi on mi knee."

"Di owner pulled di dog away, and I limped all di way home. After dat, I never went back to dat park again. Dogs in Jamaica listen when you tell dem to sit — most of di time dey run away from people."

"I love dogs," said Alaia.

"Right. Now it's definitely time for bed."

"OK," said Alaia.

She started to walk up the stairs to bed. "Thank you for the stories, Granny. I love you so much."

"And I love you even more," said Granny with a huge smile on her face.

THE END

Also by Jade Calder

The Magic Hair Stick

I am NOT Too Small

Mummy...What Is Black Lives Matter?

Betty the Bully

Professor Prophet's Miracle

The Lost Picnic

I Am Me

Gran and Grandad's Passing

My Creative Writing Book

Find out more at:
jadecalderbooks.com

www.ingramcontent.com/pod-product-compliance
Lightning Source LLC
LaVergne TN
LVHW072114070426
835510LV00002B/42